Eu...

Hippolytus

a new version by

Timberlake Wertenbaker

literal translation by
Timberlake Wertenbaker and Margaret Williamson

templetheatre

This version of *Hippolytus* was first performed at
The Riverside Studios on 24 February 2009

The Cast

Aphrodite/Chorus	BEATRICE CURNEW
Hippolytus	PAUL O'MAHONY
Nurse	ANN PENFOLD
Phaedra	KATHERINE TOZER
Theseus	DAVID BURKE
Messenger/Chorus	JUAN AYALA
Artemis/Chorus	JANE WARWICK
Chorus	SOFIA PASCHOU

Hippolytus
was produced by Temple Theatre
in association with The Onassis Programme

The Creative Team

PLAYWRIGHT Timberlake Wertenbaker

DIRECTOR Mike Tweddle

COMPOSER and
MUSICAL DIRECTOR Alex Silverman

DESIGNER Amy Levene

STAGE MANAGER and SET Mo Guiberteau

MOVEMENT DIRECTOR Bert Roman

LIGHTING DESIGNER Juan Ayala

PRODUCERS Richard Darbourne
Jane Warwick

PRODUCER FOR
THE ONASSIS PROGRAMME Helen Eastman

Temple Theatre would like to thank
Thelma Holt CBE, Jenny Topper,
Natasha Ockrent and all at Stage One,
Elizabeth Sandis, Mel Kenyon, Malcolm Taylor,
Toby Farrow, Oliver Taplin, Katie Fleming,
Edith Hall, Chris Pelling, Dr. William Allan,
The Orange Tree Theatre, Jim McCaul, Paul Purnell,
Ashley Halbach, Pandora Wheale, David King,
James Haddrell, Charlie Parker and Heather Ruck

templetheatre

RIVERSIDESTUDIOS

Temple Theatre

In 2003 Richard Darbourne, Paul O'Mahony, Mike Tweddle and Jane Warwick graduated from Oxford University with the intent to one day reconvene and set up their own theatre company. This dream was realised in 2006. Temple Theatre believes in producing fun, generous and accessible theatre. The company has won awards for its devised work throughout Europe and is based in London. *Hippolytus* is its first major commission.

The Onassis Programme

In 2005 a generous donation by the Onassis Public Benefit Foundation made possible the creation of the Onassis Programme for the Performance of Greek Drama at Oxford University. The Programme commissions, develops and produces professional work by international theatre artists inspired by Greek drama, and aims to bring the best of such work from around the world to Oxford and the UK. The Onassis Programme has worked with artists including Derek Walcott, Dominique le Gendre, Clare Higgins, Colin Teevan, The Farber Foundry, Lydia Koniordou, Struan Leslie, Seamus Heaney, Stephen Sharkey, Alex Silverman, The Clod Ensemble, Hannah Rosenfelder, and Kneehigh's Emma Rice.

Biographies

Timberlake Wertenbaker – Author

Grew up in the Basque Country and lives in London. Her plays include for the Royal Court: *Credible Witness*, *Three Birds Alighting on a Field*, *Our Country's Good*, *The Grace of Mary Traverse* and *Abel's Sister*. Among her other works are *The Love of the Nightingale* (RSC), *The Break of Day* (Out of Joint), *The Ash Girl* (Birmingham Rep), *After Darwin* (Hampstead Theatre), *Galileo's Daughter* (Theatre Royal, Bath) and *Arden City* (NT Connections). Translations and adaptations include Gabriela Preissova's *Jenufa* (Natural Perspective Theatre Company at the Arcola), Euripides' *Hecuba* (ACT, San Francisco), Eduardo de Filippo's *Filumena* (Piccadilly), Ariane Mnouchkine's *Mephisto* (RSC) and Sophocles' *Oedipus Tyrannos*, *Oedipus at Kolonos* and *Antigone* (RSC). Her libretto of *The Love of the Nightingale*, with music by Richard Mills, was performed in Perth, Melbourne and Brisbane in 2006. Her translation of Racine's *Phèdre* will open in Stratford, Ontario, in August 2009.

Margaret Williamson – Greek Consultant

Born near London, she studied at Cambridge, Toronto and London Universities. She teaches classics and comparative literature at Dartmouth College in the United States, and is the author of *Sappho's Immortal Daughters*. She previously worked with Timberlake on literal translations of *Antigone*, *Hecuba* and *Trachiniai*.

Juan Ayala – Messenger/Chorus

A trained architect, Juan specialized in physical theatre while living in Paris (Ecole Internacional de theatre Jacques Lecoq, Hippocampe mime-corporel) and later in London (Lispa). In 2001 he founded Colectivo DeCollage, a theatre group searching for a bridge between formal abstraction and the stage. In his work he combines performing and directing.

David Burke – Theseus

Stage includes most recently: *Oedipus* (National Theatre) *Afterlife* (National Theatre), *The Sea* (Haymarket), *John Gabriel Borkman,* (Donmar), *Mary Stuart,* (Donmar), *The Rivals* (Bristol Old Vic), *Wind In The Willows (Ballet)* (Royal Opera House), *Three Sisters* (A.T.G), *Further Than The Furthest Thing* (Tricycle Theatre), *Richard III/Coriolanus* (Almeida), *Copenhagen* (National Theatre, Duchess Theatre), *King Lear* (National Theatre), *New England* (RSC), *The Woman In Black* and *Pericles* (National Theatre)

Television includes: *Holby City, Midsomer Murders,* Dr. Watson in *The Sherlock Holmes Series* (Granada), *Random Quest, Spooks, Ghost Story, Dalziel and Pascoe, God's Architects, Doctors, Inspector Lynley* and *Waking The Dead, The Shackles of Sherlock Holmes, Boy Soldiers, The Regicides, Bertie and Elizabeth* and *Space Precinct.*

David has co-written a book called *Celia's Secret* with Michael Frayn (Faber).

Beatrice Curnew – Aphrodite/Chorus

Theatre includes: *Burial At Thebes* (Nottingham Playhouse/US Tour/The Rose, Kingston), *Out of Chaos,* (Berlin), *Madras House, Scenes From A Separation, Macbeth* (Orange Tree), *Improbable Fiction* (Stephen Joseph Theatre), *The Importance of Being Earnest* (National Tour), *Jump* (24hr Plays, Old Vic), *Veronika Sessions,* (Arcola), *Cyrano De Bergerac* (Minack), *Principle of Motion* (Edinburgh), *A Midsummer Night's Dream* (RNT; Platform).

Television includes*: Emergency Rescue, Glamour.*

Richard Darbourne – Producer

After three years working as a business manager in Asia for The Swire Group, Richard returned to England to establish Temple Theatre. He has been twice awarded the Stage One Bursary for Young Producers. For Temple Theatre he produced the double award winning *'Out of Chaos'* (European Tour, Blue Elephant Theatre), and *'The Really Wild Show with Brian the Clown'* (Theatre 503). Other production includes *Thyestes* (Arcola Theatre).

Richard also runs *Living Learning (www.living-learning.org)* a social enterprise company that writes and performs interactive plays for schools and community groups. He is a board member for *Upstart Theatre Company* and was identified as one of the top *Future100* Young Entrepreneurs for 2008/09.

Helen Eastman – Producer for The Onassis Programme

Trained as a director at LAMDA after graduating from Oxford University.

She is Producer of the Onassis Programme at Oxford University for whom she has commissioned and produced work since 2005. Helen is Guest Fellow in Theatre at Westminster University, Director of Live Canon and a member of the Associate Literary Panel at Soho Theatre.

Recent directing credits includes *Circus Etc* (The De La Warr Pavillion), *Dido and Aeneas* (ETO UK tour), *Hansel and Gretel* (Cork Opera House), *Fair* (Trafalagar Studios), *The Sweet Science of Bruising* (National Theatre Studio), *Cloudcuckooland* (UK tour; Total Theatre Award Nomination), *Wild Raspberries* (Glasgow Citizens Theatre), *Bug Off* (OTC), *Cure at Troy* (Delphi International Festival/ tour) and the world premiere of Julian Joseph's jazz opera *Bridgetower* (Hackney Empire and tour).

Amy Levene – Designer

Amy works as a freelance designer from her home city of Leeds, West Yorkshire. She regularly designs set and costume for touring shows and education projects with Moveable Feast

Productions, a Leeds-based company committed to producing dynamic theatre with a strong grounding in storytelling. Other recent work includes: *Love, Love, Love* (Union Chapel / Canada Fringe) and *The Package It Came In* (Etcetera Theatre Camden / Canada Fringe) *Pericles* and *Romeo and Juliet*, (St Dogmaels Abbey, Wales); and various art and design projects for regional events and festivals.

Amy studied at Lady Margaret Hall, Oxford, where she won the Cameron Mackintosh Technician's Prize.

Paul O'Mahony – Hippolytus

Paul is a founding member and a joint artistic director of Temple Theatre. For Temple he has devised and performed *Out of Chaos* and *The Really Wild Show with Brian the Clown.*

Other theatre credits include: *Leaving, Mountain Hotel, Playgoers, Nan* (all at The Orange Tree Theatre), *Othello* (RSC), *Taming of the Shrew* (Plymouth Theatre Royal), *The Suppliants* (BAC), *Amy Evans's Strike* (Courtyard), *Ice* (ETO).

Sofia Paschou - Chorus

Sofia has a diploma in both classic and acoustic guitar and classical singing. Stage includes: *How It Ended* (Edinburgh Fringe) *Singing in the Circle* (Royal Opera House) and devised work including *Forutne Cookie, Do You Like Them, The Warrant, Mutual Misunderstanding* and *Don Juan Returns from the War.*

Sofia has Assistant Directed on short films *The Girl* and *Odyssevax.*

Ann Penfold – Nurse.

Theatre credits include: *Les Liasons Dangereuses* (Theatre in the Round, Stoke), *Design for Living, The Fight for Barbara* (Peter Hall Company), *The Winslow Boy, All My Sons, The Contractor* (Oxford Stage Company), *The War of the Roses, For Services Rendered* (Old Vic), *Saturday, Sunday, Monday, In Celebration* (Chichester), *Revengers' Tragedy, Wicked Old Man, Father's Day* (West Yorkshire Playhouse), *Hamlet, Romeo and Juliet, Mrs*

Warren's Profession (Ipswich), *Ashes, As You Like It* (Birmingham and West End), *Saturday Sunday Monday* (National Theatre, West End), *Forty Years On, For Services Rendered* (Scarborough), *King Lear, The Way of the World, Mother Courage, Adam Bede* (OrangeTree, Richmond), *This Happy Breed, A Midsummer Night's Dream* (Bristol Old Vic and South American Tour).

Television includes: *Kingdom, Where The Heart Is, Sea of Souls, Can't Buy Me Love, Mile High, Casualty, Coronation Street, Cranford, Inspector Wexford, Mysteries, The Brontes of Haworth, 84 Charing Cross Road, Doctors* and, of course, *The Bill.*

Film Includes: *Family Life, Winter Sunlight.*

Ann is a graduate of Sussex University and was a member of Michael Croft's National Youth Theatre (1960-64).

Alex Silverman – Composer/Musical Director

Theatre Scores Include: *Cloudcuckooland* (UK Tour); *Romeo & Juliet, Much Ado About Nothing* (Globe); *Othello* (Salisbury Playhouse); *Richard III* (Southwark); *The Sweet Science of Bruising* (National Studio); *Crunch* (West End); *Pete & Dud: Come Again* (UK Tour).

As Musical Director/Chorus Master: *Wig Out!* (Royal Court) *Eurobeat* (West End/UK Tour); *Certified Male* (Assembly); *Bridgetower* (City of London Festival); *At the Drop of a Hippopotamus* (Pleasance/UK Tour); *David Benson's Christmas Party* (Bloomsbury Theatre/

UK Tour); *Dick Whittington* (Newbury Corn Exchange); *Swallow Song* (Oxford Playhouse); *Hamlet! The Musical* (Far Eastern Tour).

Alex has written music for BBC Radio, Channel 4 and Artsworld TV, and worked with a broad range of artists and ensembles, including recently English Touring Opera and the band Hot Chip.

Katherine Tozer - Phaedra

Stage includes: A TMA award nomination for Blanche DuBois in *A Streetcar Named Desire*, (Nuffield Theatre), *The Canterbury Tales*, (RSC, Greg Doran, Rebecca Gatward, Jonathon Munby),

Easter (Oxford Stage Company, Dominic Dromgoole), *Scapino* and *The Scarlet Letter* (Chichester), *Strange Orchestra*, (Orange Tree, Richmond), *An Inspector Calls*, (RNT/PW), *Eskimo Sister*, Southwark Playhouse, *Exiles*, (Young Vic), *The Winter's Tale*, (Bath Theatre Royal), *Far Away*, (Royal Court/Albery), *The Wrong Side Of The Rainbow*, (Donmar), *Celebration* and *Snogging Ken*(Almeida), *The Glass Menagerie*, (Exeter), *The Sea*, (Chichester), *Top Girls*, (Battersea Arts Centre) and *The Dispute* (RSC/Lyric Hammersmith).

Mike Tweddle - Director

Directing credits include *Seven Degrees of Tropical Entropy* (Union Theatre), *Out of Chaos* (Greenwich Theatre and European tour), *Oh, My Green Soap Box* (Shunt Vaults and European tour), *The Taming of the Shrew* (Tokyo Setagaya Theatre and tour of Japan), *Cloud Nine* (OFS Studio, Oxford). Assistant directing credits include *The Winter's Tale* (Shakespeare's Globe Theatre and UK tour). Mike is a founding member of Temple Theatre.

Jane Warwick - Artemis/Chorus/Producer

Jane Warwick studied History at Oxford University from 2000-3 and then trained at The Bristol Old Vic Theatre School, graduating in 2006. Credits include: Medea (Oxford Playhouse), Betrayal (Burton Taylor), The Taming of the Shrew (Tour of Japan), Cloud Nine (OFS), The Merry Wives of Windsor (Tour of Cyprus), Company (Bristol Old Vic), Beau Brummell (BBC4).

Jane has performed at the Union Theatre and at Theatre 503 with the Apathists, and on the QM2 with RADA Enterprises. In 2007 she co-wrote and performed in 'The Great Caravaggio's Travelling Circus' (BBC Radio 7 New Talent). In March 2008 she performed at the Old Vic in London as part of the New Voices' 24-hour plays.

Jane has enjoyed co-producing the Temple theatre productions in Europe and in England. Hippolytus marries her passion for education and for Ancient Greek tragedy.

Hippolytus and Us

One of the central reasons, in my view, why Greek tragedy
remains so extraordinarily powerful for us is its simultaneous
combination of the familiar and the alien, close and distant.
Here is a world, remote from us in time, place and anthro-
pology, that is, none the less, engaging with fundamental
questions about human life and experience that strike us
as uncannily immediate. And the same goes for the people.
Here are kings and princesses and slaves from a quite
different social and historical world . . . and yet their motives
and responses chime so eerily with our own, or at least with
those of people we know.

Take Phaedra. A respectable, intelligent middle-aged woman,
with time on her hands, becomes infatuated with an athletic
young man whom she sees around the house every day. The
fact that he is stainless, ascetic, confident in his superiority
to ordinary folk, makes him all the more fascinating and
sexually attractive. The woman is shocked by the strength of
her own erotic urges, she does her best to suppress them,
and to hide them from everyone else; she does not want to
harm her marriage and her children from that marriage. But
she is making herself ill, subject to something close to delirium.
And, in the end, she cannot conceal her obsession from a
close female confidante. Things begin to go terribly wrong,
despite her best efforts to save the situation. Does all that
sound implausible, remote, the experience of a world quite
other from ours?

Theseus is a leader, who has to live up to people's expectations
of him as an active, exceptional man: he does his best in the
demanding world of power and responsibility. He can be
quick to anger, especially in matters that touch his personal
integrity and pride. He has a bastard son, whom he has
brought up with every privilege, a clean-living promising

young prince, a potential leader in his turn. And then it turns out – according to good, though false, evidence – that this paragon has been trying to seduce his beloved wife, even that he has forced her to have sex. She has killed herself from shame. There is nothing incomprehensible or foreign about his fury, his disgust, and his hasty, impatient desire to make his treacherous son pay dearly. What is different from our world, and more like folk tale, is that he has the fortune to be the son of a god, and that his father has granted him three wishes. Perhaps we should count ourselves fortunate that we do not have such dangerous 'blessings'?

Many modern readers of the play think they recognise Hippolytus, or his type, and dislike him pretty strongly. He is the prig, holier-than-thou, the no-alcohol, no-meat, no-sex exercise freak. He is not modest, but proud of his superiority and his incorruptibility; and Euripides gives him a group of loyal friends, young men who admire his lifestyle and values. In the end, though, it is not the lifestyle that marks out Hippolytus, it is his attitude to sex, and hence to all manifes-tations of sexuality. He is repelled, nauseated by what he regards as the lust, the fumblings, the mucousy orifices, blind rubbings in the dark, bodily excretions and odours. Is Hippolytus' longing for purity really so incomprehensible? Life *would* be a lot cleaner without sex – it would also, most of us would say, be less worth living. So Hippolytus represents an extreme attitude, but not one that is unequivocally bad, let alone one that deserves an untimely and horrible death. In my view, the play is more powerful if Hippolytus is allowed some understanding, and is seen to balance by opposition the more easily recognisable extreme of Phaedra.

There are powerful and incompatible gods in this play. Hippolytus reveres the virgin huntress Artemis; Phaedra cannot resist Aphrodite, voluptuous god of sexuality. Too many critics jump to the conclusion that this is a tragedy which exemplifies the total power of the gods, reducing humans to mere pawns, victims of higher powers. Aphrodite '*makes* Phaedra fall in love', they say. Are they saying that she would not have fallen in love if she had not had her erotic wiring interfered with? Do any of these alleged pawns do or express anything that contradicts their human dispositions, anything that would be implausible without supernatural interference?

What makes the play 'tragic', in my view, is not to do with 'Fate' or inevitability, it is the sight of struggling humans trying to do the right thing, trying to live according to their sincere values, and yet still failing into disaster. Things can turn out horribly badly despite our best efforts. Life is not always like that, thank goodness, but it can be. Euripides confronts us with that life-possibility without shrinking. Things do not go bad in *Hipploytus* because of vicious behaviour, there are no villains, it is not a story of good versus evil, or of god versus anti-god. It is much more powerful than a mere morality tale – and much more like life in all its complex reality. If anyone is a 'villain' in the play, it is, as Theseus proclaims in its closing lines, the goddess of sex, Aphrodite. But what would life be without her? 'There's the rub', as another bard put it.

OLIVER TAPLIN

Oliver Taplin is an Emeritus Fellow of Magdalen College, Oxford, a Director of the Archive of Performances of Greek and Roman Drama, and author of a number of books on Greek drama and theatre.

Euripides
Hippolytus

a new version by

TIMBERLAKE WERTENBAKER

*literal translation
by Timberlake Wertenbaker
and Margaret Williamson*

faber and faber

First published in 2009
by Faber and Faber Limited
74–77 Great Russell Street
London WC1B 3DA

Typeset by Country Setting, Kingsdown, Kent CT14 8ES
Printed in England by CPI Bookmarque, Croydon, Surrey

A CIP record for this book
is available from the British Library

ISBN 978-0-571-25067-7

2 4 6 8 10 9 7 5 3 1

Characters

Aphrodite
Goddess of Love

Artemis
Goddess of Chastity and of the Hunt

Theseus
King of Athens and Trozene, father of Hippolytus

Phaedra
wife of Theseus, stepmother of Hippolytus

Hippolytus
illegitimate son of Theseus and an Amazon queen

Nurse

Servant

Messenger

Chorus of Hunters

Chorus of Women

HIPPOLYTUS

Trozene.

Aphrodite on stage.

Aphrodite
　Very powerful
　And famous
　On earth
　As well as in heaven,
　I am called the Cypriot:
　Also known as Aphrodite.
　When:
　Those who live between the Black Sea to the east and
　　the boundaries of Atlas to the west, I mean those
　　who have access to sunlight, that is, human beings,
　When these worship me and respect my power
　I look after them.
　But I crush
　Anyone who takes a lofty attitude towards me:
　The gods too enjoy celebrity and honours.
　And I will quickly demonstrate the truth of my words.
　See over there
　The young shoot of the Amazon –
　The bastard son of Theseus –
　Brought up by the wise Pitheus
　There – Hippolytus,
　Alone of all the denizens of this city of Trozene
　He calls me the worst of the gods.
　He's not interested in sex
　Won't even contemplate marriage,
　The only god he worships is Artemis

That lilywhite virgin sister of Apollo.
And he claims that in his considered judgement
She is the greatest of all the gods.
And so he gallops through the green forests
Always in the company of the chaste goddess
Decimating the wild animals of this land.
Social climbing his way into the high society of
    immortals.
I might allow that, why should I care?
But not his failings towards me:
For those, I'll have my revenge this very day.
I don't even need to do much because I advanced the
    matter some time ago.
You see, Hippolytus once came from Trozene to
    Athens to view some holy mysteries and his father's
    royal wife, Phaedra, took one look at him and was
    seized by the most violent desire.
Which was what I had intended.
Some time later, Theseus slaughtered the entire family
    of the Pallantides, his rivals for power in Athens,
    and he had to leave the city to purge himself of all
    that blood.
And he sailed to this land of Trozene
To the hunting forests of Hippolytus.
He sailed with Phaedra
Who, goaded by sharp spasms of desire, moans
But will not speak.
She's dying
And no one can name her fatal disease.
But it won't work out that simply.
I'll make Phaedra's passion known to Theseus.
And then the father will kill this young man who
    dared to declare war on me.
Phaedra will keep her good name but she'll have to
    die as well

8

Collateral damage of my revenge.
I can't put her suffering above mine, can I?
Not when I'm seeking the satisfaction of seeing justice
    done.
But here he comes
The child of Theseus
That very same Hippolytus
He's finished his hunt for the day.
Time to leave.
He's followed by a great crowd of hunters
All shouting praises to the pure goddess,
To Artemis.
Well:
Hippolytus does not sense the gates of death opening
    before him
He doesn't know this is the last day he will ever see.

*Hippolytus enters with his hunting companions,
singing.*

Hippolytus
Hepesth' aedontes hepesthe.
Follow me, friends, follow me
And sing
To the goddess:
Heavenly Artemis
In whom we trust.

Chorus of Hunters
Potnia potnia semnotata,
Almighty goddess,
Glorious child of Zeus,
Xaire xaire moi,
Glory be to you
Virgin most venerable
In your house of gold
Queen of heaven.

Xaire moi o kallista,
Oh most beautiful and
Blessed virgin
Artemis!

Hippolytus
For you:
This garland
Woven from the grasses of a pure meadow
Which the shepherd dares not defile with flocks
Nor does the blade of the scythe ever touch it,
Undisturbed untouched meadow
Where the bee sucks the cool spring dew
Sprinkled with the water of rivers
Whose source is reverence.
Only those whose unschooled nature
Is moulded by self-control,
Those with temperance
Flowing in their veins –
Only they can pluck its holy grass.
But for all others, the impure:
No trespassing.
Beloved mistress,
Take this garland
Woven by a reverend hand
And bind your golden hair.
I, alone of all human beings,
Have this honour
To cohabit with you to speak to you
Always your voice in my ears
Even if I may not see you
And let me complete the course of my life
In this way always.

Servant
My lord –
I reserve the term master for addressing the gods –

Would you be willing to accept a word of advice from
   someone who wishes you well?

Hippolytus
   I would appear most unwise if I didn't.

Servant
   Do you know the law established among human beings?

Hippolytus
   Which law? Why the question?

Servant
   It is to hate those who give themselves airs and are
   generally rude.

Hippolytus
   Quite. Putting on grand airs brings trouble to human
   beings.

Servant
   And good manners always find favour?

Hippolytus
   They cost little and bring great benefits.

Servant
   Is this not the same for the gods?

Hippolytus
   Yes, if humans have the same rules as the gods.

Servant
   How is it then that you fail to address a revered
   goddess?

Hippolytus
   Which one? Take care your tongue doesn't trip you.

Servant
   This goddess. Aphrodite, who guards these gates.

Hippolytus

I am chaste and so address her from a safe distance.

Servant

And yet she is proud and celebrated among humans.

Hippolytus

She is especially wonderful at night and as such
doesn't interest me.

Servant

My dear child, we must honour all the gods.

Hippolytus

With men as with gods: some appeal, others don't.

Servant

I wish you luck and the good sense that is necessary.

Hippolytus

Go into the house, friends, and look after the meal.
A good hunt demands good food.

Rub down and feed the horses so I can exercise them
later.

To the Servant:

As for that Aphrodite of yours, I wish her good day.

He goes. The Servant addresses Aphrodite.

Servant

We will not imitate the young but I will pray to you,
mistress, venerable Aphrodite, in a language fit
for slaves.

But it is necessary to show understanding towards
someone who because of his youth is wound too
tight and speaks foolishly and with hubris. Pretend
not to hear. Gods need to show more wisdom than
humans.

*He leaves as the Chorus of Women from Trozene
come on.*

Chorus of Women
Water
Drawn from the deep recess of the ocean
Cascades down a rock face
Into a pool
Where we plunge our pitchers.

There – a friend of mine
Had soaked her purple robes
And spread them out to dry
On the shoulder of a sun-baked rock.

And it was she who told me of my mistress
Her anguish
How Phaedra barricades herself inside
Enclosed in darkness
Shrouds her head in black cloths
And wastes away.

Three days without food
A secret torment
Storms through her
Tosses her into that black harbour
Death.

What god possesses you, youthful Queen?
Is it Pan of the night terrors?
Or Hecate?
Have you been bewitched by the wild Chorybants?
Did the fierce mountain mother call out to you?
Or
Did you neglect to worship the huntress Dictynna,
Goddess of wild things?
Did you forget to make an offering of water
As she roamed the sand bars

The moist eddies of the sea?
Or
Is it your husband Theseus
Leader of the Erechtides
Has he strayed into a secret bed
And abandoned yours?

Or did some sailor
Coming from your native Crete
Sail into the safe harbour of this land
Bringing such news
That it felled you, Queen,
And bound you to your bed in pain?

And women anyway are always helpless
Confounded by the female constitution
Pains of childbirth the madness
How well I remember
The torment coursing through my womb
But I called on Artemis
Goddess of childbirth
And she always came.
I was lucky
Thanks be to the gods.

But here comes the nurse
Holding up Phaedra's frail body
Dark cloud over her brow.
What's happened?
I long to know
What eats away at the Queen
Drains her face of all colour.

Nurse
To be human is awful and to be ill, hateful.
What must I do, what can I do for you?
Here is the light, here is the air,

You insisted on coming out here
But you'll soon ask to go back inside.
You change so quickly, nothing gives you ease.
You don't like what's in front of you,
What's somewhere else is always more desirable.
It's really better to be ill oneself than to look after
    the ill.
The first is straightforward the other full of grief:
Hard work for the hands and even more for the mind.
And yet, there's nothing better than life itself.
The rest is shrouded in darkness, veiled by clouds,
And so we love what glitters on this earth
We know nothing of any other world.
We drift to the echoes of strange tales.

Phaedra

Hold up my body, straighten my head
The strength of my limbs is melting away.
This head-dress is too heavy
Take it off
Spread my hair over my shoulders.

Nurse

Show some courage, child, and don't contort your
    body so painfully.
Try to bear your illness with calm and a noble reserve.
It's the lot of human beings to suffer.

Phaedra

Aiai.
If only I could drink pure water
From a fountain dripping with dew
Lie under tall poplars
Stretch myself out on the woven grass
Of a soft meadow
And rest.

Nurse

Dear child, don't talk like that
Don't say such things in public
Words that seem carried by a mad wind.

Phaedra

Take me to the mountains
Let me run into the forest
Through the stiff pine trees
Where the sharp-jawed hounds chase spotted deer.
Oh yes, by the gods.
I too would give tongue,
Take in my hand the Thessalian javelin,
Draw it back over my shoulder,
Throw:
It whizzes past my flowing hair.

Nurse

What's all this about hunting dogs
And flowing streams?
Why don't you drink from the fountain just outside
    the palace?
It has excellent water.

Phaedra

Mistress of the salt marshes
Sacred Artemis
Guarding the sandy racetracks by the shore
Let me go down there,
Listen to the beat of galloping hooves
And tame the high-spirited foals.

Nurse

First you're off to the mountains hunting wild beasts,
Now you're down by the seaside taming horses.
I'd need to be a sorcerer to guess
What god has yanked you off course and pulls you
    this way and that.

Phaedra

What am I doing?
The reckless impulse of some god drives me
Whips away my good sense.
Feu feu tlaimon
Sweet nurse cover my head again,
Hide my shame.
What have I said?
Tears pour from my eyes,
My face burns.
The disgrace –
Terrible to thrash about in madness,
Best not to be conscious – yes – to die.

Nurse

I'm covering you.
But what about me? When will death cover my body?
Life has taught me many things
For example
Human beings should be measured in their attachments
And never disturb the marrow of their soul.
Any attachment should be easily dissolved,
Tightened and loosened at will because when one soul
    suffers for two people
As I do for Phaedra
That's a lot of pain.
They say that conduct that is too exacting creates
    more problems than rewards.
It's actually unhealthy
And so in my book excess comes way down after
    moderation.
Nothing in excess I say
And all wise people will agree with me.

Chorus

Old woman, faithful nurse, we see Phaedra's unhappy
    state but we don't know what the disease is.

Nurse

I don't know either, she won't say.

Chorus

Can she explain how it began?

Nurse

Nothing. She remains silent.

Chorus

How weak she seems, unravelled.

Nurse

She hasn't eaten for three days.

Chorus

Is it some malevolent fate or does she want to die?

Nurse

She's fasting to death.

Chorus

Her husband doesn't mind?

Nurse

She hides her grief.

Chorus

Doesn't he see it in her face?

Nurse

He's gone away on some pilgrimage.

Chorus

Can't you make her speak so you may understand the disease and the wanderings of her mind?

Nurse

I've tried everything. I'll try again. Listen and you'll hear to what lengths I'll go for my unfortunate mistress.

To Phaedra:

Come, dear child, loosen that frown from your brow
 and change the course of your thoughts. I will try
 to use more skilful words.
Child, if you are suffering from a disease that ought
 not to be made public, then here are women who
 can help ease matters.
If, on the other hand, your distress can be mentioned
 in front of men, then speak quickly and we can
 refer the matter to doctors.
Well then? Why are you still silent?
Don't remain silent, child, argue with me if I haven't
 spoken well, or agree with me if I have.
Say something.

To the Chorus:

Women, these efforts are hopeless.
She wasn't softened by words before and she won't
 be persuaded now.

To Phaedra:

You ought at least to know this:
You may be as stubborn as the sea
But if you die you betray your children.
They will inherit nothing from their father
And your children's master will be the son of the
 galloping Amazon,
That bastard who parades himself as legitimate heir
You know well who I mean
That Hippolytus –

Phaedra

Oh you gods!

Nurse

That hit the mark!

Phaedra

You're killing me, *maia*, I beg you never to mention that man again.

Nurse

You see, you can still think clearly. And yet you refuse to help your own children by sparing your life.

Phaedra

I love my children but I'm caught in the whirlwind of a different fate.

Nurse

Do you have blood on your hands, child?

Phaedra

My hands are clean, my heart is soiled.

Nurse

Has some enemy put a curse on you?

Phaedra

A friend destroys me, despite himself, despite myself.

Nurse

Theseus has done something wrong?

Phaedra

May I never wrong him.

Nurse

Well, what's this terrible thing driving you towards death?

Phaedra

Let me be, my failure is not yours.

Nurse

But I will have failed because of you.

She clasps her knees and hands.

Phaedra

What are you doing, taking my hands by force?

Nurse

And your knees, I will never let go.

Phaedra

You will die if you hear. And yet, I derive some glory from my actions.

Nurse

How can you hide a noble secret despite my prayers?

Phaedra

I want to extricate myself from something shameful by showing courage.

Nurse

You will show more courage if you speak.

Phaedra

Go away and let go of my hand.

Nurse

Not until I have the gift I deserve.

Phaedra

Very well. Out of respect for your supplicating old hands.

Nurse

I'll stay silent and wait for your words.

Phaedra

Unlucky mother, what a love you had.

Nurse

Because she fell in love with that bull?

Phaedra

And you, poor sister, married to Dionysus.

Nurse

Why are you insulting your whole family?

Phaedra

I am the third. I die the most unfortunate.

Nurse

What are you saying?

Phaedra

It's not new. It happened then –

Nurse

I still don't know anything.

Phaedra

What is this thing which men call love?

Nurse

Nothing sweeter, child, and painful too.

Phaedra

I only know the pain.

Nurse

You're in love? With what man?

Phaedra

That one. The one, son of my husband, born of the
Amazon.

Nurse

Hippolytus!

Phaedra

You named him. I did not.

Nurse

What have you said?
You've destroyed me.
Women, I cannot live –
To tolerate the intolerable

The day is hateful, the light ugly,
I'll throw my body off some cliff.
Farewell,
I am no longer
Because here are people who are good but want
   something evil.
Aphrodite I see is not a goddess but a mega-goddess
She has destroyed this woman, this household and me.

Chorus

Aies o, eklues o
Anekousta tas
Turannou pathea melea threomenas.
Did you hear?
Did you take in?
The Queen uttering words
Which ought never to have been heard.
Io moi feu feu
O talaina ton d'algeon.
Humans feed on so much pain.
Queen,
You are ruined
You've brought such harm into the light
What will happen now, throughout this day
As Aphrodite's plots work themselves out
Inexorable and –
No longer obscure?
Unhappy daughter of Crete.
O talaina pai kresia.

Phaedra (*now very firm and rational*)

Women of Trozene,
During the long hours of night I have often reflected on
   how a human life is destroyed.
It seemed to me that human beings do not come to
   harm when they follow their own sense, because
   on the whole they judge well.

However, we may know and recognise what is right
    and not put it into practice.
Some out of laziness and some because they prefer
    other pleasures rather than what they know is
    good. Pleasures like chatter, leisure and then there
    is a kind of reverence, a modest uncertainty, let's
    call it a sense of shame,
Which can be a good thing or a bad one, depending –
Sometimes the same words lead in opposite directions –
Having pondered these things I decided that no poison
    would make me conduct myself in a manner that
    my own judgement condemned.
And so, as soon as I was crippled by this love,
I considered how best to bear it.
I decided to keep quiet, hide the disease,
Since the tongue may be good at giving advice but
    often brings harm to the person speaking.
I chose to bear my folly with dignity and to triumph
    over it by means of a sober mind.
But
When all those resolutions failed to overcome the
    power of Aphrodite, I decided it was time to die.
This seemed the best possible outcome.
I could not bear the infamy that goes with the disease,
    the act –
I'm a woman and therefore already a general object
    of contempt.
And I hate those women who mouth pieties and
    indulge their passions in secret.
Tell me, Aphrodite, how do they face their husbands
    without fear that the walls of their house, the
    accomplices of their dark acts, will not one day
    betray them?
This is what kills me now, this fear I will dishonour
    my husband and the children I have from him.

How will they live in glorious Athens, free, proud
of their mother?
Having rotten parents can turn men into slaves.
There is one thing that is as valuable as life itself and
that's a just and a good mind. Time will eventually
reveal those who are evil as clearly as in a polished
mirror and I do not want to be counted among
those people.

Chorus

Feu feu.
Virtue is full of good things and brings with it an
excellent reputation.

Nurse

Mistress,
Your situation seemed terrible to me earlier – it
frightened me, but now I think I was foolish.
Second thoughts are always better.
There is nothing unusual or strange about what's
happened to you: the anger of a goddess strikes
you.
You love.
What's so terrible about that?
Most humans do the same.
And you say you want to die because of this love?
Does that mean that anyone who loves their neighbour
has to commit suicide?
The god is irresistible.
If you yield, she'll be gentle with you but if you
resist
Thinking yourself above such things
She'll seize you and punish you.
Aphrodite roams through the air,
Skims the ripples of the sea
All things feed on her

She scatters love on earth and it's to her we owe our
birth, our lives.

Remember how Zeus burned for Semele and also how
the goddess Dawn whisked the human Cephales
into the domain of the gods.

They did this because of love.

They are gods, they live in the heavens and they
accepted the circumstances of their defeat. They
even grew to like their affliction.

Why should you not bear it as well?

You would have to be born in unusual circumstances
and under different gods to be exempt.

How many sensible people when they see their
marriage go wrong look the other way?

How many fathers are complicit in their children's
misbehaviour?

It's wise to allow what's not good to escape your notice

And anyway it's not necessary for human beings to
work too hard at being perfect.

No one measures to the very last inch the roof
covering their house.

Now that you've plunged into this fate, don't think
you can swim out of it.

You can count yourself lucky if you have a little more
good than evil in your life

And so my child, turn away your dark thought, forget
your pride –

Because it is hubris to try to best a god.

Dare to love.

A god wishes it.

Turn this ill to your benefit. There are incantations,
words that charm, and a remedy for your disease
will soon appear. I can tell you one thing more:
men wouldn't get anywhere if we women weren't
so resourceful.

Chorus

    Phaedra, her words are more expedient than yours, but
        in these circumstances it's your behaviour I praise.
    However, my praise may be more painful for you than
        her words.

Phaedra

    It's words like hers that destroy well regulated houses
        and cities. One ought not to use words that are
        pleasing to the ear but rather words that help keep
        us on a straight road.

Nurse

    You don't need fine speeches, you need the man.
    Let us look at the situation and name it for what it is.
    If your life weren't in danger, if you were still chaste,
        I wouldn't lead you on to pleasure
    But the real struggle is to keep you alive, and for that
        I will do anything, however distasteful.

Phaedra

    Your words are disgraceful.

Nurse

    They may be disgraceful but they'll do you more good
        than the words you glory in.
    Better the act if it will save you than drape yourself in
        noble sentiment and die.

Phaedra

    Stop, please. No more. My soul is already frayed by
        desire. If you weave honeyed words into the shame
        I want to escape, I'll unravel altogether.

Nurse

    If that's what you really want, fine. But if you've
        already gone astray in your heart then do what I say.
    I have in my house charms which will remedy the
        disease without shame or damage to your mind.

But you must not lose your courage.

Phaedra
What will you do? Use a drug, a drink?

Nurse
Seek the benefit, don't ask questions.

Phaedra
You're too clever for me . . .

Nurse
What is there to fear?

Phaedra
Something you might say to Hippolytus.

Nurse
It will be fine, child, I'll manage the situation well.

Turning to the statue of Aphrodite:

Only come to my help, Aphrodite.
I'll share the rest of my thoughts with the women
    indoors.

The Nurse leaves.

Chorus
Eros, eros, ho kat'ommaton
Stazdeiz pothon –
Desire
Drips longing into the eyes
Binds the soul
Hostage
And injects sweet pleasure.

Desire
When you dance
Your frenetic steps
To the chaotic rhythm of pain

28

Come not my way
Desire
Please pass me by.

Neither fire
Nor the force of exploding stars
Matches in power
Aphrodite's weapons
Of mass destruction
Launched by Eros
God's child god
Desire.

You can try prayers
Sacrifice oxen
Sacrifice everything
Through all of Greece
To no avail
If you do not honour
Desire
Destruction where his missiles fall
Defoliation
Rubble.

So many stories
Remember Iole
Gambolling like a young foal
Never knew the bit, the bite of marriage,
Until
Desired by Heracles
She tries to escape
Olympic naiad mad bacchae
Kidnapped by Aphrodite
A bloody wedding choked with the smoke
Of smouldering buildings
And for the marriage feast
A requiem for her city

Wiped out by Heracles
The man who yokes her
Unhappy girl, what a grim wedding.

Aphrodite
Breathes flames of destruction
Everywhere.
And yet look
How delicately she flits
Like a sunlit bee.

Phaedra
Silence!
I'm ruined!

Chorus
What is it? Something terrible in your house?

Phaedra
Let me find out whose voices I hear inside.

Chorus
I'll keep quiet. This is ominous.

Phaedra
Io moi aiai.
Misfortune and now pain.

Chorus
Tina throeis audan?
Tina boais logon?
What makes you so fearful? Speak!

Phaedra
Ruined.
Come close.
Listen to what sounds fill my house.

Chorus
You're closer, you can tell us

Enepe d'enepe moi
Ti pot eba kakon.

Phaedra
The son of the Amazon
Hippolytus
Shouts at the nurse, insults her.

Chorus
Axan men kluo, safes d'ouk exo.
What I hear is faint, tell me the meaning.

Phaedra
He speaks of the matchmaker from hell betraying her
master's bed.

Chorus
You are betrayed, friend, betrayed by a friend.
Ti soi mesomai?
Your secret comes to light
And your ruin is complete.

Phaedra
Omoi ego kakon.
She spoke of my condition
And destroyed me.

Chorus
Kind but not wise. And what now? What will you
do? There is no solution.

Phaedra
Only one: to die as quickly as possible.

Hippolytus bursts out of the house, followed by the
Nurse.

Hippolytus
Mother Earth and you clear radiance of the sun,
What repulsive words still swarm in my ears!

Nurse

Quiet, dear child, your shouts will be heard.

Hippolytus

How can I keep quiet after the terrible things I've
heard?

Nurse

I beg you by your gracious right hand –

Hippolytus

Take your hand away! Don't touch me or my clothes!

Nurse

Don't destroy me.

Hippolytus

Why? Since you insist you've done nothing wrong.

Nurse

What I said was not meant for everyone.

Hippolytus

What is good can be heard by anyone.

Nurse

Child, you swore, do not dishonour your promise.

Hippolytus

My tongue swore, my mind did not.

Nurse

Will you destroy those close to you?

Hippolytus

No one who does wrong can be close to me.

Nurse

You must forgive. It is natural for humans to fail.

Hippolytus

Oh God, why did you bring into the sacred light of

day this counterfeit evil, this plague for all mankind,
women?
If you wanted to keep the human race going you
should have found a way to do it without women.
It should have been possible to go to a temple with
some gold or silver or bronze and buy some embryos,
each one priced according to its worth, and then
these could be brought up in houses free of women.
Women ruin us. Notice how quickly a father gives his
daughter a dowry so he can be rid of her.
And the poor man who takes this poisonous plant
into his house starts buying adornments for his
idol, he buys her trinkets, dresses her in fineries
and eventually destroys the wealth of his house.
As for the in-laws, when they behave tolerably, it's
usually because the woman is useless in bed. But if
he loves the woman and it's the in-laws who are
useless, he has to put up with them because of his
love. The clever women are the worst. Keep me
from ever marrying a woman who thinks more
than is strictly necessary. It's in minds of the clever
ones that Aphrodite finds the most accessible inroads.
At least the stupid ones don't have the resources
to do much damage.
If by misfortune you do have a woman in your house
then make sure she has no servants. Let her have
the company of wild beasts who can't hear or
speak. Because women make evil plans and the
servants execute them.
And that's what you've done. You come to me,
suggesting I corrupt the sacred bed of my father.
How can I purge myself of your words? Streams of
pure water cannot wash the filth from my ears.
How could I ever behave in such a way when I am
pure, and ignorant of these things?

Only one thing saves you, woman, and that's my
   respect for the gods. You took me off guard and
   made me swear I would reveal nothing. Now I am
   bound by my word or I would have told Theseus.
As it is, I'll leave this house until he comes back but
   beware, I'll watch you closely to observe with what
   brazenness you greet my father, since I've been
   subjected to it myself.
May you all die. I'll never have enough of hating
   women – even though they say I repeat myself.
They are evil. Let them learn some self-control or let
   me be allowed at all times to trample them with my
   words.

Hippolytus leaves.

Phaedra
   Talanes o kakotuxeis
   Gunaikon potmoi.
   Misery and misfortune allotted to all women.
   A noose of words strangles me
   How can I loosen it?
   Where can I hide?
   Which god, which mortal will help me now?
   I've been hurt to the limits of life
   Kakotuxestata gunaikon ego,
   Most unfortunate of women, yes, I.

Chorus
   Feu feu.
   The plots of your servant have failed badly.

Phaedra (*turning to the Nurse*)
   Good for nothing conwoman
   Destroyer of friends,
   May Zeus my ancestor blast you with lightning
   Erase you from this earth.
   Didn't I order you to keep quiet

34

About matters now blazing in the light, revealed to all?
But you couldn't hold back
And now you've even robbed me of an honourable
    death.
What language do I have now?
Hippolytus in his anger will tell his father
And his tutor Pitheus and the whole country
Will be awash with stories of my shame, this disgrace
    humiliation.
I hope you die – you and all those who say they want
    to help their friends and instead lead them astray.

Nurse

Mistress, you reproach me for my mistake.
Pain snaps at you, blurs your insight.
But I have something to say. Listen, please:
I nursed you, I love you, I wish you well, I was trying
    to help you, cure your illness. I didn't succeed. If
    I had, I'd be called a wise woman.
Only when they are successful are people called
    intelligent.

Phaedra

How dare you try to placate me? Words of syrup –
What you've done!

Nurse

We're wasting words now, it's still possible to be
    saved, child.

Phaedra

Stop. Your advice was useless before and your actions
    evil.
Get out, look to your own affairs. I'll manage this
    situation myself. Leave me. Go!
And you, inhabitants of Trozene, only grant me this:
Cover up with silence everything you've heard here.

35

The Nurse leaves.

Chorus

I swear by the venerated Artemis never to reveal your troubles.

Phaedra

I will not dishonour my Cretan home, my name. I will not face Theseus with this shame emblazoned on my face.

Chorus

What are you planning now?

Phaedra

To die.

Chorus

Don't speak of such things.

Phaedra

Don't give me bad advice. And you, Aphrodite, help me bring my life to its close. You must be pleased now, since you chose to destroy me with the bitter, deadly poison of desire.

But I will hurt someone else with my death. He too will suffer from my disease and be forced to learn some self-control.

Phaedra leaves.

Chorus

Let me slip into the deep crevasse of a high mountain
Or join incognito a flock of migrating birds
Perhaps surf the high waves of the sea
Where Phaeton's daughters mourn with amber tears.
Take me to the shore where the magic apples grow
To the ocean's edge beyond which no sailor goes
To the fold of sky which Atlas lifts.

Near the bridal chamber of Zeus sparkle fountains
    of ambrosia
And there the fecund earth feeds the prosperous gods.

Woe to the white-winged ship when it ploughed the
    waves
To convey my mistress from a happy home
To this badly arranged marriage.
No joy here
When she left her Cretan land
For famous Athens.

Already the omens were bad.
Remember how the sailors
Had to attach those ropes
In the port of Piraeus
Those tresses of ropes.
Only then did she step onto the shore
Over the ropes.

And then Aphrodite felled her
With this terrible disease,
Entangled her in desire.
And now in that bridal chamber
The rope dangles
She fits the rope
Around her white neck
Shamed by her illness
She saves her good name
Frees herself from the gnawing obsession
Of her heart
Desire.

The Nurse rushes on.

Nurse
    Help! Run to help. The mistress has hanged herself.

Chorus

It is done.
Feu Feu.
She hangs
By the rope.

Nurse

Bring a sharp knife to cut the rope. Hurry!

Chorus

What shall we do? Can we cross the threshold of the
palace and free Phaedra from the rope?
There must be young attendants already there. It is
always safest not to interfere.

Nurse

Stretch out the corpse.
What a bitter homecoming for my master.

Chorus

She is dead.
They are laying out the body.

Theseus enters, a garland on his head.

Theseus

Citizens, what are these cries coming from the palace?
And why no welcome for the weary pilgrim that
I am? Has Pitheus died? He was old but it would
be sad to lose him.

Chorus

Theseus: it is not the old but the young you must
mourn.

Theseus

My children? Has one of them died?

Chorus

They live but their mother is dead.

Theseus
What? My wife? How?

Chorus
She tied a rope
And hanged herself.

Theseus
From grief? In what circumstance?

Chorus
That's all we know. We only came this instant to
lament your troubles.

Theseus throws off his garland.

Theseus
This crown mocks my unlucky pilgrimage.
Release the bolts, open the doors – let me take in the
bitter sight of my wife
Whose death destroys my life.

Phaedra's body is brought out.

Chorus
Io io talaina meleon kakon
Epathes
Aiai tolmas.
Who, unhappy woman, blighted your life?

Theseus
I will seek the darkness
Beneath the earth,
Deprived of you, dying myself, desperate,
Your death pulls other deaths in its wake.
What fate brought your life to a halt?
Will someone tell me what happened or do I feed
a horde of useless servants?
Here is an empty house, orphaned children.
You flew from my hands, fragile bird

Swooped deep down into Hades
You – the best of women
Ever to look up towards the flaming sun,
At the dancing stars.

Chorus

I mourn with you, tears flow down my cheeks, but
    I shudder at the thought of the suffering still to come.

Theseus

There's a small tablet hanging from her wrist.
Is it something new? A last prayer? A request?

To Phaedra's body:

Rest assured, my love, I will never bring another
    woman into this house.
But I can't take my eyes off the seal of her gold ring.
Let me untie the scroll
And see
What the tablet wishes to say.

Chorus

A new calamity falls,
Adds itself to the growing pile.
Why, oh God, do you wish to destroy this house?

Theseus

Oimoi
Woe on top of woe,
Beyond words beyond endurance.

Chorus

What is it? Say – if you are willing to speak to me.

Theseus

This tablet shouts,
Shouts such things – cannot be ignored.
How can I flee the weight of these evils,
This destruction?

Chorus

Your words prepare us –
What misfortune?

Theseus

No. I will not silence this horror.
Hippolytus. Hippolytus, without respect for the
   sacred eyes of the god
Forced himself soiled my bed raped her –
Father Poseidon, lord of the sea, you once offered
   me three wishes –
This is my first wish:
Execute my son. Now.
If you meant those wishes to be mine
Let Hippolytus not survive this day.

Chorus

Lord, by the gods, take back your prayers. You may
   discover one day that you made a mistake.

Theseus

Never. I'll throw him out of this land and one of two
   fates will strike him down.
Either Poseidon will dispatch him quickly down to hell
Or, exiled from his country, he will wander, a sad
   refugee,
Hanging on to the miserable hold of a living death.

Chorus

Here comes your son just in time.
Forgo your anger, Lord, consider what is best for
   your house.

Hippolytus enters.

Hippolytus

I heard your shouts, Father, and came here quickly.
But I don't yet know the cause of your sorrow. I hope
   you will tell me.

Ah, but what's this? Your wife. I left her only recently.
What happened? How did she die? Please tell me,
Father. I wish to learn of this from you.

Theseus is silent.

You're silent. Silence has no place in the midst of
sorrows. It is not right, Father, for you to hide your
misfortune from your friends – from one who is
even closer to you than a friend.

Theseus
Oh mankind, full of failure and so useless,
You teach so many crafts, you're capable of so many
discoveries,
But there is one thing you do not know and have
never grasped:
How to teach sense to those who are mindless.

Hippolytus
Indeed, it would be a very wise man who could teach
sense to the senseless. But this is no time for
sophistries, Father. I fear your troubles are throwing
your words off course.

Theseus
Human beings need sound judgement to distinguish a
true friend from a false one. Indeed, men themselves
ought to have two voices: one which always told
the truth, and the other one which could gabble as
it pleased. The just voice would always check the
false one, and thus no one would ever be deceived.

Hippolytus
You words don't make sense, Father.

Theseus
Alas for the human heart. Where is it going? How
much more daring and perversion can it hold?

These swell from generation to generation, each
one going further than the last one. Soon God will
have to invent a whole new earth simply to house
the wicked.

Turns to Hippolytus, points him out.

Look at this man,
Born my son,
Who stands convicted of violating my marriage.
Come here, stand before your father
Look into my eyes.
Is this you, the remarkable man who consorts with
    the gods?
The man of wisdom untouched by evil?
Keep boasting – I cannot believe the gods are stupid.
You call yourself a vegetarian, flaunt yourself as a
    whirling dervish, soaking up the vapours of
    mystical teachings.
But you have been caught out.
I call on all men to keep clear of people like you.
You hunt people down with your holy words and
    cover your shameful acts in secrecy.
She is dead, did you think this would save you?
It is her very death which convicts you, you the evil one.
What oaths what arguments are more powerful than
    this dead body?
No way for you to wriggle out of your guilt now.
Of course, you'll say that she hated you and that the
    bastard is by nature the enemy of the legitimate.
But she would have made a bad bargain if she'd been
    willing to pay for her hatred of you with her most
    precious life.
Or will you say that folly is more common in women
    than in men?
But I know that young men are no more steady than
    women when Aphrodite brings turmoil to their hearts.

The fact that they're men only helps exonerate their
  acts.
But why am I even arguing with you when this body
  lies here, the most credible of witnesses?
Get out of this land
Now.
Stay away from Athens and any other country under
  my rule.
And if I allow you to get away with what you've done,
  then let them say I never slew monsters, I never
  punished offenders, but only talked about it. Let
  them say I am not Theseus.

A pause.

Hippolytus
  Father, terrible passions rage through your heart, but
    this matter which provokes such fine words is not
    fine when looked at clearly.
  Now I am not good at speaking in front of a crowd,
    I am better before my peers and a few other people.
    This is as fate has willed it and anyway, it's not
    always the best people who sing fine speeches before
    a crowd. However, now, in these circumstances,
    I must loosen my tongue and speak.
  I will start by your accusation against me which you
    thought would stun me into silence.
  Father, do you see this earth, this sunlight?
  There is not a man, even if you deny it now, who has
    more self-control than I do.
  In the first place, I know how to respect the gods. And
    I have acquired friends who would not even
    consider doing wrong and who would be ashamed
    to tempt any of their friends to evil.
  I would never scorn these companions, Father.
    Whether I'm with them or far away, I am always
    the same.

44

And there is one thing I have never touched and yet
you would convict me of this.
My body is chaste to this day
I have never been to bed with anyone.
I have no knowledge of this activity except what I hear
about and see in pictures,
And I've not even any great desire to see those because
I am chaste to the marrow of my soul.
If my self-control doesn't convince you, show me how
I could have been corrupted.
Did she have the most beautiful body of any woman?
Or did I expect to become your heir by acquiring your
wife?
I would have had to be completely senseless. Well,
you'll say, power is attractive. Perhaps, but not to
anyone with good sense. But absolute power corrupts
those who have it absolutely. Yes, but I did not have
such power.
I like to shine in sport, to come first in the Olympic
games, but I am quite content to take second place
in the city with my friends and enjoy the good
fortune I already have. A sense of safety brings
greater rewards than being all-powerful.
I have only one thing left to say:
If only I had a witness to vouch for me –
If she were still alive, if you combed through our
actions in detail,
Then you would know who was the guilty one.
As things stand, I swear, by Zeus who holds all oaths
sacred, and by the full expanse of this earth,
That I never touched your wife, nor did I want to,
nor did I think of it.
May I die, without fame, without a city, without a
home, an exile wandering the earth, and may the
earth and the sea refuse my body burial
If there is anything bad in my nature.

I don't know if she killed herself out of some fear –
I am not allowed to say more –
She achieved self-control without really having it,
But I who have it have not made good use of it.

Chorus

You have said enough to ward off all accusations.
It is no small matter to swear by the gods.

Theseus

Does this man think he's a sorcerer who can lull my
soul to sleep with sweet spells and the display of
a gentle temper?

Hippolytus

It's rather your conduct that surprises me, Father. For
if you were the kind of son you say I am and I your
father I would have killed you, not threatened you
with mere exile.

Theseus

Death is too easy a way out for transgressors. You
will be exiled from your own country, a refugee
on inhospitable soil, and you'll drink the dregs of
a bitter existence.

Hippolytus

What will you do? Won't you allow time to reveal
more information? Will you drive me out?

Theseus

Behind the highest mountains and beyond the edges
of the sea, so hateful is your face to me.

Hippolytus

You'll throw me out without sworn testimonies, some
evidence or proof, without a trial, without at least
consulting soothsayers?

Theseus

This tablet condemns you beyond reasonable doubt.
Let the birds fly overhead, and as for those
twitching birdwatchers who are supposed to tell
us what to think, I wish them a good day.

Hippolytus

Oh gods! Why can't I open my mouth – defend myself?
Why am I being destroyed by you whom I revere?
No – I can't break my promise, and anyway, it wouldn't
do any good.

Theseus

Your grandiose piety will be the death of me! Get out
now!

Hippolytus

Where can I go? What house will take me in when
I'm under such suspicion?

Theseus

Go to a place which welcomes men who corrupt
women while pretending to be the guardians of the
house.

Hippolytus

My heart is breaking. How can I not shed tears when
I appear a criminal, seem so to you?

Theseus

You ought to have shed tears earlier when you dared
to rape your father's wife.

Hippolytus

If only the walls of the house could speak and testify
that I am not an evil man.

Theseus

You call on witnesses who can't speak. But the dead
in their silence declare you guilty.

Hippolytus

If I could stand apart and see myself I would weep at the evils I am suffering.

Theseus

Yes, you're very good at honouring yourself instead of honouring your parents.

Hippolytus

Unhappy mother, bitter birth,
May no friend of mine ever be born illegitimate.

Theseus

Take this man away. It's been some time since I've declared him an exile.

Hippolytus

Let no one dare lay a hand on me! You yourself, since you desire it, can push me out.

Theseus

I will if you don't obey, and I will be pitiless.

Hippolytus

It is decided then. And yet – I know things – can't say them –
Artemis, most beloved of the gods, fellow hunter and companion of all my hours,
I must flee from this land and keep out of Athens.
Farewell, Trozenian plain,
The most blissful place in which to be young.
This is the last time I look upon you.
Come, companions, escort me out of this land.
Even if my father cannot see this,
You will never encounter a man with more self-control.

Hippolytus leaves with his companions.

Chorus

When I contemplate the gods
Their concern for us
My heart swells with hope
But when I observe the acts of men
All my hopes fade.
Despair as I try to understand, fail.
Events twist and turn, fold over
And man's life is eternal wandering.

I pray to the gods to grant me this:
Prosperity and a heart untouched by pain.
May I see clearly but without rigidity
And may I adapt to changing circumstances
And in this way find good fortune.

I feel no ease
When I see the brightest star of Athens,
Indeed throughout Greece,
Chased out of his land by an enraged father.

Your chariot will no longer course around the lake
And the muse will desert your father's house.
We will no longer hear your voice
Weave around the lyre strings.
Artemis will find her temples empty.
No more garlands tressed with love,
No more competition
Among the young girls who hope to marry you.
All life snuffed out
Because of your misfortune
And I will spend my life mourning yours,
A life that is no longer a life.
Oh sorrowful mother,
You gave birth to no purpose
I rage at the gods,

Io Io,
And you, Graces
Dancing enlaced
In your winding farandoles
Why didn't you protect him?
Why did you send this poor youth
Who has done nothing wrong
Out of his land
Out of his house?
But here comes the servant of Hippolytus in great haste.
He's running towards the house.
Is he angry? Sorrowful? I can't tell.

Messenger

Where might I find the ruler of this land? Is he in the
house?

Chorus

He's coming from there now.

Messenger

Theseus,
I bring news of concern to you, to the citizens of
Athens and to the citizens of Trozene.

Theseus

Has some calamity swept through both cities?

Hippolytus

Hippolytus
Is no more – or barely so.
He breathes, but his life hangs in the balance.

Theseus

What killed him? Or who?
Did he rape someone's wife as he did his father's?

Messenger

His team of horses destroyed him – and your prayers
to Poseidon.

Theseus
> Thank you, Poseidon, for granting me my wish.
> How did he die? How did the trapdoor of justice
> > slam down on this man who humiliated me?

Messenger
> We were grooming our horses down by the wavelapped
> > shore. And we were weeping because we had just
> > been told you'd expelled Hippolytus from this
> > country and that he would never return.
> He joined us on the shore, we all mingled our tears –
> > a harmony of grief.
> In time, he restrained himself and spoke:
> 'Why this distress? I must obey my father. Men,
> > harness the horses to my chariot since I am no
> > longer welcome in this city.'
> We were all eager to work for him and the horses
> > were soon ready.
> He seized the reins, leapt into the chariot and fitted
> > his feet on the chariot's footholds.
> First he spoke to the gods, raising his hands:
> 'Zeus, may I die if I am not a good man.
> And may my father one day know how he has wronged
> > me, either when I am dead or even still alive.'
> And then he took the whip into his hand and struck
> > the horses.
> We followed on foot as he took the road south to
> > Argos and Epidauros.

> As we were making our way towards the promontory
> That reaches into the Saronic gulf
> We crossed a deserted stretch of land.
> Suddenly
> An echo rumbles from the depths of the earth
> As if the thunder of Zeus had exploded underground.
> Ominous
> Horrible

The horses lift their heads, ears pointing to the sky
And we shuddered with fear
Wondering where the sound came from.
And then we saw the sea.
A wave towered up
Stood vertical
Attached itself to the sky
Obscuring the shore and the islands beyond.
It swelled higher
Foam bubbling
And then with a roar it crashed on the shore.
Three waves, and the third
Disgorged a bull,
Monstrous indescribable,
And his bellow engulfed the earth.

Fear shot through the horses and the master,
Skilled horseman that he is,
Took the reins in both hands and leant back like
    a sailor,
Pulling at the oars,
But they clamped their bits,
Ignored the soothing hand of their master
And bolted with the chariot.
Whenever he tried to guide the horses onto flat land
The bull would rear in front
And the horses turned
Maddened with terror.
When the horses made for the rocks
The bull followed behind
Until the horses tripped and the chariot keeled over,
Throwing the axle onto the rocks.
A splinter of wheels
Chaos,
And he

The son you cursed,
Entangled in the reins,
Was dragged over the rocks
His head crashing over the stones
His flesh torn, splayed open.
He cried to them, painful to hear his cry:
'Stand still, horses, you were reared in my stables,
Don't destroy me now,'
And then:
'Who will come and help me,
This good man,
Cruelly cursed by my father?'
We wanted to help but our feet seemed to drag
Until finally, I don't know how, he was free of the reins
And lay still, breathing, barely.
The horses galloped off
And the monster bull vanished into the folds of the
    rock.

I am only a slave in your house, King,
But I cannot obey you in this:
I cannot believe your son is bad,
Not if the whole race of women hanged by the neck,
Not if all the tablets in the world accused him.
I know him to be good.

Chorus

So many evils welded together
Fate is irresistible and there is no escape.

Theseus

If my hatred for Hippolytus makes me take pleasure
in your account, respect for the gods and sadness
for a child of mine hurts me. And so I feel neither
joy nor sadness. I feel nothing.

Messenger

> What shall we do with the body? Bring it here? It's
> up to you. But my advice would be not to act
> savagely towards your unfortunate child.

Theseus

> Bring him here: I will confront him again with the
> rape he denied. He will be convicted once and for
> all by my words and by this punishment of the god.

Artemis appears.

Artemis

> You there:
> Theseus,
> Son of the noble Aegeus.
> It is Artemis herself addressing you.
> I command you to listen.
> You have murdered your son, you have transgressed,
> your mind was soiled by your wife's lies and you
> believed them.
> You were persuaded by what was unclear but the
> retribution you will suffer will soon be clear enough.
> *Ate.*
> You should scurry beneath the earth as far down as
> the gates of hell to hide your shame,
> Or try flying high in the air to unload your pain:
> There is no longer any place for you in the company
> of good men.
> Now hear, Theseus, the range of your evils,
> Even though the telling of it will cause you nothing
> but grief.
> I have come for this: to display the purity of your
> son's heart so that he may die with his reputation
> intact.
> And I will reveal the passions that shook your wife
> but also her brave struggle.

This is what happened, Theseus:
That goddess who is hated by all of us who are chaste,
That Aphrodite
Was the one who whipped your wife into a frenzy of
    desire
For your son.
She fought hard in her heart to resist Aphrodite
But she was undone by the machinations of her nurse,
Who revealed to your son – under oath to repeat
    nothing – your wife's disease.
And because he was a pious man he did not forswear
    his oath when you accused him.
Phaedra was afraid you would find out the truth and
    convict her.
And so she wrote the lies you read to destroy your
    son.
And you believed her.

Theseus
    Oimoi.

Artemis
    Does my account begin to gnaw at your heart? There's
        more, listen, and then you can shout your pain.
    You were granted three wishes by Poseidon and
        instead of using these against your enemies you
        used the first one against your own son.
    Your Ocean father had to grant your wish but he
        judges you evil, and so do I.
    You didn't wait for a sign, further proof, you didn't
        ask questions, cross-examine or consult soothsayers,
        but let loose this curse against your own son.
    And you murdered him.

Theseus
    Goddess, let me die.

Artemis
It was Aphrodite's will.
Her anger, her revenge against your son.
I had to stand back as no god can oppose the will of
another god.
If I did not respect this law I would never have allowed
her to humiliate me by destroying the man I love
most among mortals.
Your ignorance attenuates your guilt because Phaedra,
by killing herself, avoided questions and persuaded
you.
Grief for you but grief for me too.
It is when men are bad that we happily destroy them,
their families and their possessions,
Not so now.

Chorus
Here he comes,
His young flesh in ruins,
Golden hair streaked with blood.
A god seized this house
In his fist
And crushed it like a toy.

Hippolytus is brought in.

Hippolytus
Aiai
Hold up my mangled body
Pain shoots through my head
I am destroyed.
Hold me gently.
Stop now
And let me rest,
I am dying – unjust chastisement of an unjust father
And my horses fed from my own hands
Killed me.

Who's that on my right?
Zeus, do you see this?
Cursed by a father's mistake
I leave this life, I, the most godfearing of men
Who surpassed everyone in self-control.
Aiai this pain!
The unhappy curse of my father
Wipes out my life.
I, always innocent, who never hurt anyone,
Worked hard, fulfilled my duties
Towards all men –
For nothing.

Aiai this pain
Comes now, comes again.
Let me go!
Come death, natural healer,
Or let a sword
Slit my throat my life.
Io moi moi ti fo?
What can I say
To sever this life from this pain,
Black-night cloak of Hades
Cover me now
I beg you
And let me rest.

Artemis

Unhappy youth,
The goodness and nobility of your heart destroyed you.

Hippolytus

Divine fragrance . . . a sudden ease of body . . .
Is Artemis here? In this place?

Artemis

She is here, poor youth, your very own beloved goddess.

Hippolytus
Have you seen what's been done to me?

Artemis
I see it, but the gods cannot cry.

Hippolytus
You've lost a follower, a devoted hunter.

Artemis
I will cherish you even in death.

Hippolytus
Your horseman, the guardian of your sacred images . . .
No more.

Artemis
Aphrodite the spoiler planned it so.

Hippolytus
And so it was that goddess who killed me?

Artemis
She disliked how you honoured her, she hated your
self-control.

Hippolytus
She destroyed all three of us, I see it now.

Artemis
Yes, your father, his wife, and now you.

Hippolytus
Then I must also mourn my father's misfortune.

Artemis
Tricked by the wiles of the goddess.

Hippolytus
Grim circumstances, Father, you suffer too.

Theseus
I am done for, child.
No solace for me ever again.

Hippolytus
I pity you more than myself because you were in error.

Theseus
If only I could die in your place, my child.

Hippolytus
Poseidon's bitter gift . . .

Theseus
If only it hadn't escaped my lips.

Hippolytus
You were so angry you would have killed me anyway.

Theseus
The gods had fractured my reason.

Hippolytus
If only human beings could punish the gods!

Artemis
Let that be.
Aphrodite's actions will not go unpunished,
Even when you are buried deep beneath the earth.
And now you, Theseus, son of Aegeus,
Take your child in your arms, embrace him.
You destroyed him unwillingly:
Men make mistakes when the gods decree it.
Hippolytus: do not hate your father
Because this was the fate apportioned to you.
And so farewell, I cannot defile my eyes with the sight
    of a corpse.

Hippolytus
Goodbye, blessed one,

How easily you leave me . . .
Beloved goddess, farewell.
I have always obeyed you
And so I will forgive my father now.
Hold me, Father, straighten my body.

Theseus
Child, what are you doing to me?

Hippolytus
The gates of the underworld open before me.

Theseus
You leave me with bloodied hands and a soul in
torment.

Hippolytus
No, Father. I absolve you of this death.

Theseus
You release me from my guilt?

Hippolytus
I call upon Artemis as my witness.

Theseus
Beloved son, what nobility of spirit you reveal to
your father.

Hippolytus
Farewell, Father, and again farewell.

Theseus
Alas for your piety and your good heart.

Hippolytus
May you find the same in your legitimate children.

Theseus
Don't leave me, child, make an effort to live.

Hippolytus
My endurance is spent, cover my face with your robes.

Theseus
Great city of Athens, high walls of Trozene, what
a man you're losing.
And what sorrows for me now for ever.
Aphrodite: *you* unleashed this
Very powerful evil.
I will remember.

Chorus
These sorrows came to our city unforeseen.
Tears will now flood through the land
Because the sufferings of the great
Take up so much space.